BALL BUSTERS™
FOOTBALL

Bob Moog

UNIVERSITY GAMES

San Francisco • Maastricht • Sydney

ACKNOWLEDGMENTS

Publisher: Kirsty Melville

Editorial Director: Erin Conley

Content Editor / Fact Checker (Brainteasers, Secret Identities): Maria Llull

Designers: Laurel Lane, Michelle Hill, Jeanette Miller, Lynn Gustafson

Content Creator (Word Searches): Cherie Martorana

Special thanks to Suzanne Cracraft, Peter Crowell
and Kristen Schoen for their invaluable assistance.
© 2005 University Games

First edition published in 2005

Spinner Books, a division of

University Games Corporation
2030 Harrison Street San Francisco, CA 94110

University Games Europe B.V.
Australielaan 52 6199 AA Maastricht Airport, Netherlands

University Games Australia
10 Apollo Street Warriewood 2102 Australia

Library of Congress Cataloging-in-Publication Data on file with the publisher.

ISBN: 1-57528-979-2

Printed in China.

2 3 4 5 6 7 8 9 10 – 09 08 07 06

INTRODUCTION

The Ball Busters™ series proudly pairs our favorite sports with a scintillating mix of brainteasers, trivia, word puzzles and word searches. Each book in the series celebrates a different popular sport, featuring its stats and stars of yesteryear and today.

In *Football*, we poke fun at the team nicknames and honor football's greatest practitioners and their accomplishments. We revisit the exploits of Joe Namath, the pluck of the early Packers and the outrageous stunts of the Oakland Raiders. Now, with hundreds of questions, facts and figures at your fingertips, you and all your friends can see how much you really know about the only Sunday past-time more popular than going to church.

I hope that you score a touchdown every time you pick it up and play.

Happy punting,
Bob Moog

4

- 12 is my favorite number.

- After my sporting days,
  I tried acting.

- My team's colors were green
  and white.

- I finished my career with the
  Los Angeles Rams.

- I was the first to wear
  white shoes.

- My nickname was
  "Broadway Joe."

I AM JOE NAMATH.

UNDER THE CENTER

Rearrange the letters below to make the first names of three NFL quarterbacks from the 1960s.

RABT

NFAR

NSYON

Bart (Starr)
Fran (Tarkenton)
Sonny (Jurgenson)

1. What vast retail complex now stands on the former home of the Minnesota Vikings, Bloomington's Metropolitan Stadium?

2. In 1974, Joe Namath starred in a controversial TV commercial for Beautymist®, endorsing what kind of product?

3. Which NFL team won the first Super Bowl in 1967?

7

4. What Ohio city shares its name with a province in China and is home to the Football Hall of Fame?

5. In football, numbers 1-19 are reserved for which two types of players?

6. What famed 1960s football coach asked, "If winning isn't everything, why do they keep score?"

Solutions:
4. Canton 5. Quarterbacks and kickers 6. Vince Lombardi

- I won the Super Bowl in Oakland, CA.

- I belong to the "Fear of Flying Club."

- Many people think I have a bad temper.

- My favorite letters are X and O.

- I named my own All-Star team in 2004.

- You have heard me on *Monday Night Football*.

9

I AM JOHN MADDEN.

LORDS
OF THE RING

BALTIMORE (2001, 1971)

CHICAGO (1986)

DALLAS (1996, 1994, 1993, 1978, 1972)

DENVER (1999, 1998)

GREEN BAY (1997, 1968, 1967)

KANSAS CITY (1970)

MIAMI (1974, 1973)

N.Y. GIANTS (1987, 1991)

N.Y. JETS (1969)

NEW ENGLAND (2005, 2004, 2002)

OAKLAND (1981, 1977)

PITTSBURGH (1980, 1979, 1976, 1975)

RAIDERS (1984)

SAN FRANCISCO (1995, 1990, 1989, 1985, 1982)

ST. LOUIS (2000)

TAMPA BAY (2003)

WASHINGTON (1992, 1988, 1983)

Search for the words listed in all CAPS.

WORD SEARCHES

```
            O  B  D
         S  H  Z  A  I  S  Y
      X  R  A  L  Q  L  K  M  A  N  G
      H  J  R  L  N  X  T  U  L  B  S  D  W
   A  I  N  Y  L  Y  T  I  C  S  A  S  N  A  K
   X  R  O  M  A  P  S  M  C  N  P  N  O  S  L
L  Q  K  P  G  D  B  T  O  F  U  M  D  D  H  B  V
X  F  O  J  G  A  N  N  R  X  A  A  L  A  I  E  V
L  J  D  G  X  I  J  C  A  E  N  T  T  D  E  N  V  E  R
W  T  D  H  J  V  W  N  I  L  E  V  K  O  N  G  U  A  T
A  I  H  A  H  A  C  M  G  H  G  R  U  B  S  T  T  I  P
L  R  O  P  I  A  N  Y  R  C  N  G  R  I  O  L  D
G  Q  F  S  I  N  K  N  F  S  T  E  J  Y  N  E  G
   C  C  M  N  B  E  L  F  X  D  R  W  Y  V  G
   O  V  L  S  T  L  O  U  I  S  F  S  E  M  L
      H  E  J  A  Z  I  A  H  S  B  Z  M  N
      K  X  M  P  R  T  T  A  T  P  N
         D  L  X  O  C  Y  U
            J  E  T
```

7. At every Super Bowl since 1971, the NFL Commissioner presents what trophy to the owner of the winning team?

8. Name the only player in the NFL who has won the Super Bowl MVP award three times.

9. Former pro football player Howie Long once co-starred in a Radio Shack TV ad campaign with which *Desperate Housewives* cast member?

12

FLEW THE COOP

I grew up in Chicago in the 1940s and flew to St. Louis in 1964. Then I bid farewell to St. Louis and headed west in 1987.

What kind of bird am I?

13

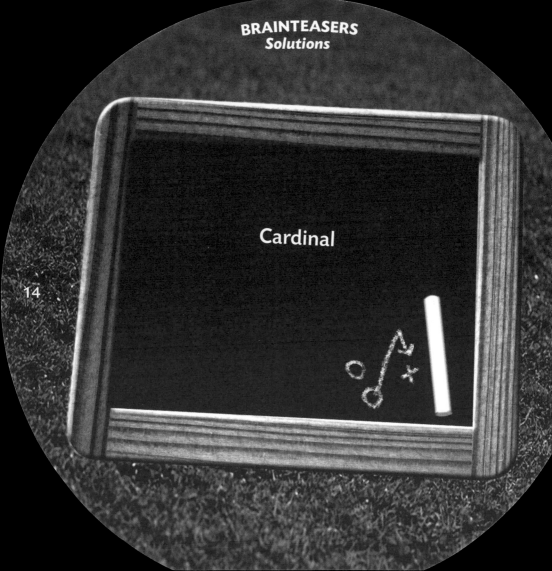

Cardinal

10. What is the official team name for the Buffalo Bills' cheerleading squad?

11. What college football coach gave the "Win One for the Gipper" speech?

12. A "chop block" is an illegal block that occurs in what region of the body?

15

16

- There is a city named after me.

- Pop Warner called me the greatest.

- I was the first president of the NFL.

- My name is "Bright Path" in my native language.

- Burt Lancaster played me in the movies.

- I was a decathlon and pentathlon champion in the 1912 Olympics.

I AM JIM THORPE.

• My legendary stars include Joe Perry and Frankie Albert.

• Jack be nimble, Jack be quick, Jack jumps over my stadium.

• I won four Super Bowls in nine years.

• My favorite colors are red and gold.

• I brought Montana to California.

• I share my name with 19th century prospectors.

I AM THE SAN FRANCISCO 49ers.

SUPERMEN

Troy AIKMAN (1993)

Marcus ALLEN (1984)

Ottis ANDERSON (1991)

Terry BRADSHAW (1980, 1979)

Tom BRADY (2004, 2002)

Deion BRANCH (2005)

Larry BROWN (1996)

Terrell DAVIS (1998)

Richard DENT (1986)

John ELWAY (1999)

Desmond HOWARD (1997)

Dexter JACKSON (2003)

Ray LEWIS (2001)

Joe MONTANA (1990, 1985, 1982)

Jerry RICE (1989)

John RIGGINS (1983)

Phil SIMMS (1987)

Emmitt SMITH (1994)

Kurt WARNER (2000)

Doug WILLIAMS (1988)

Steve YOUNG (1995)

Search for the words listed in all CAPS.

WORD SEARCHES

```
              F   B   Q
          C   W   N   Z   G   O   H
      J   E   C   M   T   A   U   F   X   M   Z
      U   M   S   F   C   S   T   A   Y   S   R   X   B
  T   S   T   O   P   C   V   M   R   G   I   Q   C   J   Y
  G   P   F   L   G   A   A   R   J   W   M   L   Y   N   Z
S   K   T   Z   U   E   W   H   Y   A   T   M   E   E   O   C   D
D   X   S   U   U   L   V   Q   O   T   V   S   W   T   S   Y   C
L   X   I   P   S   S   V   K   I   B   W   I   A   I   K   M   A   N   X
T   W   Q   Q   P   Y   I   C   T   B   R   A   D   S   H   A   W   S   I
I   U   H   D   W   O   B   V   J   R   I   A   R   A   N   I   L   R   T
  G   J   R   E   U   G   I   A   A   C   W   N   D   U   L   E   W
  Z   O   R   I   N   S   H   C   D   E   A   E   C   G   L   G   K
      U   O   O   G   T   H   K   Y   T   R   L   Z   H   I   C
      S   W   K   X   G   T   S   N   S   N   L   H   H   W   G
          B   L   W   M   I   O   O   Y   E   A   M   V   D
              M   A   Y   M   N   W   O   R   B   I   H
                  R   S   W   S   G   D   V
                      Z   C   G
```

13. What stadium is home to the Green Bay Packers?

14. Who played football coach Hayden Fox in the long-running TV series *Coach*: Gerald McRaney, Craig T. Nelson or Rutherford T. Grant?

15. What record field goal distance is held by kickers Tom Dempsey (of the New Orleans Saints) and Jason Elam (of the Denver Broncos)?

20

Solutions:
13. *Lambeau Field* **14.** *Craig T. Nelson* **15.** *63 yards*

WHO OWNS WHO?

Match the owner or former owner
to the team:

1. Al Davis
2. Bill Bidwell
3. Jack Kent Cooke
4. Georgia Rosenbloom
5. Art Rooney

A. Pittsburgh Steelers
B. Oakland Raiders
C. Washington Redskins
D. St. Louis Rams
E. Phoenix Cardinals

1-B
2-E
3-C
4-D
5-A

22

16. Name the kicker whose field goals provided victories in two of the three Super Bowl wins for the New England Patriots.

17. The coveted Vince Lombardi Trophy stands 22 inches tall, weighs seven pounds and is made entirely of what?

18. On March 21, 1946, halfback Kenny Washington became the first African-American player to join the NFL, signing with what pro team?

19. College football's highest honor is presented annually by the Downtown Athletic Club and is better known by what name?

20. What two NFL teams has head coach Jimmy Johnson led?

21. Which running back ran for 1000 yards in a season eight times and led Pittsburgh to four Super Bowl titles?

24

- My heroes include The Snake.

- I moved from one Coliseum to another.

- I won the "Heidi" game.

- In 1986, Tom Flores was my coach.

- My logo has a man wearing an eye patch.

- My colors are black and silver.

25

I AM THE OAKLAND RAIDERS.

IF THEY COULD
SEE ME NOW

ADRENALINE RUSH

A-TEAM

BENGALS

BOMBSHELLS

BUFFALO JILLS

CHARGER GIRLS

COWGIRLS

GOLD RUSH

RAIDERETTES

SABERKITTENS

SAINTSATIONS

SEAGALS

SIDEWINDERS

STEELERETTES

THE FLAMES

THE ROAR

THE SIRENS

TOP CATS

WARDOLLS

WILD BUNCH

26

Search for the words listed in all CAPS.

```
            Y  W  T
         A  K  R  S  I  O  S
      K  N  D  V  L  Q  L  L  P  R  I
      M  L  O  R  L  S  Q  L  E  D  C  W  J
   N  I  S  N  E  T  T  I  K  R  E  B  A  S  K
   P  M  T  H  N  W  J  T  R  U  V  R  U  T  F
S  I  I  S  K  A  O  T  H  E  S  I  R  E  N  S  M
U  J  B  R  S  L  R  I  G  R  E  G  R  A  H  C  S
Z  P  M  V  S  A  I  N  T  S  A  T  I  O  N  S  D  H  D
H  O  C  M  F  M  N  R  F  R  O  T  S  L  A  G  A  E  S
B  S  P  F  Z  S  E  T  T  E  R  E  L  E  E  T  S  D  B
   W  U  R  H  M  R  B  H  D  E  R  L  L  K  D  C  E
   B  A  R  V  U  U  Q  E  N  H  E  T  J  U  O  N  W
      P  R  D  C  S  Z  F  I  T  D  U  K  W  G  A
      P  L  D  L  H  Q  L  W  D  I  M  G  A  R  T
         B  I  O  O  M  A  E  T  A  I  L  C  F
            C  Y  L  G  M  D  G  R  S  U  S
               M  L  E  I  L  B  T
                  S  S  M
```

27

28

22. What celebrated American author wrote *The Great Gatsby*, but didn't make the cut when he tried out for the Princeton University football team?

23. What term describes the area behind the offensive line where the quarterback is protected by his blockers?

24. After losing four Super Bowls, what NFL team won the Super Bowl in 1998 and 1999?

RIDDLE ME THIS

Name the football position and four players that Big Daddy was talking about when he said, "That Young one has a cap and star in Montana."

29

Quarterback
Steve Young
Joe Kapp
Bart Starr
Joe Montana

30

25. As of 2005, which NFL team has never won the Super Bowl: the Oakland Raiders, the New York Jets, the Seattle Seahawks or the Kansas City Chiefs?

26. What former pro football player starred in a classic 1979 Coca-Cola® TV commercial?

27. What television football commentator, and former NFL star won the Super Bowl MVP award back-to-back in 1979 and 1980?

Solutions:
25. Seattle Seahawks (Raiders won '77, '81; Jets won '69; Chiefs won '70)
26. Mean Joe Greene 27. Terry Bradshaw

32

• I was born in
  Pittsburgh in 1933.

• I broke Y.A. Tittle's
  record.

• I was considered the
  greatest quarterback
  of my era.

• I lead my team to two
  national championships.

• I looked good in blue
  and white.

• I brought fame to #19.

I AM JOHNNY UNITAS.

- I led my team to six division titles and two Super Bowl wins.

- I played my entire career with one team.

- Vince Lombardi was my coach.

- My team listened to me from 1956-1971.

- I was the MVP of Super Bowls I and II.

- I coached the Green Bay Packers after my playing career.

33

28. What is the official name of the San Francisco 49er cheerleaders?

29. In the 1993 movie based on a true story, what college did Rudy dream of playing for?

30. In the NFL Europe league, teams are awarded four points for field goals kicked from over how many yards: 40, 50 or 60?

34

DYNASTY TIMES

In the early 1990s, what team had a tailor, some sanders, a lot, and threw rice every Sunday?

San Francisco 49ers
(John Taylor, Deion Sanders,
Ronnie Lott and Jerry Rice)

31. In college ball, what yard line does the kicking team kick off from?

32. What color flag does an AFL coach throw down if he wants to challenge an official's call?

33. What pro quarterback made a cameo appearance in the 1998 comedy *There's Something About Mary?*

Solutions:
31. Their own 35-yard line 32. Red 33. Brett Favre

34. What color is the flag NFL official's throw onto the field when calling a penalty?

35. What is the total length of a regulation NFL football field, including both end zones?

38

36. On a football field, inbound lines are also referred to as what?

39

- I was born in 1903.

- I had my best years with the Chicago Bears.

- I started out as a runner and finished up on defense.

- I went to college at University of Illinois.

- My nickname is "the Galloping Ghost."

- I was an early NFL star.

I AM RED GRANGE.

YOU MAKE
THE CALL!

CHOP BLOCK

CLIPPING

DEAD BALL

DELAY OF GAME

ENCROACHMENT

FACEMASK

FALSE START

FIELD GOAL

GROUNDING

HOLDING

ILLEGAL SHIFT

INFRACTION

INTERFERENCE

OFFSIDES

OUT OF BOUNDS

PERSONAL FOUL

ROUGHING

SAFETY

SPIKING

TOUCHDOWN

40

Search for the words listed in all CAPS.

```
                    E  F  S
                 B  X  C  T  D  D  Q
              R  O  U  G  H  I  N  G  J  N  L
           T  Z  G  N  I  D  N  U  O  R  G  P  F
        S  G  N  I  D  L  O  H  O  H  Y  E  N  I  T
        E  I  P  E  X  Y  W  U  B  P  R  N  K  N  O
     L  D  P  L  P  M  E  E  G  F  S  H  O  F  T  U  G
     X  I  D  F  L  H  H  F  F  O  H  O  I  A  E  C  N
  O  L  S  E  L  I  E  S  C  N  T  L  K  T  C  R  H  I  P
  C  R  F  A  U  D  E  G  A  A  U  C  I  C  E  F  D  K  G
  C  H  F  D  T  D  E  L  A  Y  O  F  G  A  M  E  O  I  O
  X  O  B  R  I  F  Z  D  L  R  R  V  R  A  R  W  P
  W  G  A  C  O  E  S  B  G  S  P  C  F  S  E  N  S
     P  L  U  H  N  P  A  A  O  H  P  N  K  N  T
     S  L  P  X  O  I  U  F  Z  A  I  I  E  C  I
        I  E  H  D  E  C  H  E  R  L  F  Z  E
           C  F  A  L  S  E  S  T  A  R  T
              U  H  Z  I  X  I  Y
                 N  L  K
```

41

37. How many seasons did the Raiders play in Los Angeles: 10, 13 or 16?

38. Purposely throwing the ball without a realistic chance of completion is referred to as what in the NFL?

39. In the NFL an offsides penalty is a loss of how many yards for the team at fault?

Solutions:
37. 13 38. Intentional grounding 39. Five yards

Like a Rolling Stone

(or I Sat on the Roof and Kicked Off the Moss)

What team exemplified the expression, "A rolling stone gathers no moss," when one of its stars joined the Raiders in 2005?

Minnesota Vikings (when they traded Randy Moss to the Oakland Raiders)

40. What type of football, played in the Ivy League, did the British Army bring to North America?

41. What US president threatened to make football a federal crime after 18 players were killed while playing in 1905?

42. What former NFL Vikings and Giants quarterback went on to co-host the 1970s TV show *That's Incredible!*?

45

46

- In the 1960s, I defined NFL toughness.

- I was All American at University of Illinois in 1965.

- I played in eight straight Pro Bowls.

- I was the prototypical linebacker.

- Chicago is my kind of town.

- My career ended in 1973 with a knee injury.

I AM DICK BUTKUS.

- In 1989, I hit a home run and scored an NFL touchdown in the same week.

- I am the only player to play in a Super Bowl and a World Series.

- I came out of retirement in 2004 to play for Baltimore.

- I finished as the greatest cover corner in NFL history.

- I won Super Bowls with the Cowboys and the 49ers.

- My nickname is "Prime Time."

47

I AM DEION SANDERS.

NOT IN OUR HOUSE!

ARROWHEAD Stadium	METRODOME
CANDLESTICK Park	PAUL BROWN Stadium
DOLPHINS Stadium	RALPH WILSON Stadium
EDWARD JONES DOME	RAYMOND JAMES Stadium
FORD Field	RCA DOME
GEORGIA DOME	SOLDIER FIELD
GIANTS Stadium	SUN DEVIL Stadium
GILLETTE Stadium	THE COLISEUM
HEINZ Field	
LAMBEAU Field	

48

Search for the words listed in all CAPS.

WORD SEARCHES

```
            M   X   B
        M   E   P   G   R   T   S
    K   Z   T   C   I   A   S   L   X   C   S
    A   W   R   I   L   G   L   U   D   D   R   V   Q
M   N   O   S   L   I   W   H   P   L   A   R   X   T   P
C   D   X   E   A   Z   M   F   Z   Y   B   J   U   T   O
F   O   K   T   N   R   O   F   E   M   M   S   R   L   T   G   L
M   L   T   T   O   C   O   A   O   F   H   O   P   O   R   E   S
E   G   E   S   I   J   R   S   N   I   H   P   L   O   D   W   E   R   I
B   I   Y   Q   P   D   S   D   P   E   M   O   D   A   C   R   N   L   G
S   A   Z   R   X   R   J   E   M   O   D   A   I   G   R   O   E   G   A
    S   I   K   R   A   P   K   C   I   T   S   E   L   D   N   A   C
    E   O   B   M   W   D   A   E   H   W   O   R   R   A   A   G   U
        F   E   L   D   H   O   Z   Y   L   I   F   L   P   G   O
        S   L   C   E   S   U   N   D   E   V   I   L   B   O   A
            I   M   U   E   S   I   L   O   C   E   H   T   N
            M   I   U   A   E   B   M   A   L   W   Q
                G   H   H   U   E   M   D
                    Q   J   G
```

43. What NFL all-star bowl is held each year in Honolulu, HI and features players from the AFC and the NFC?

44. What is the official length of an NFL regulation football?

45. Which of New York's two pro football teams actually play their home games in New York City?

50

AUDUBON SOCIETY

Zack decided to become a bird watcher.

*What four places does he go to
on Sunday afternoons to see Ravens,
Seahawks, Eagles and Cardinals?*

51

Baltimore (Ravens)
Seattle (Seahawks)
Philadelphia (Eagles)
Tempe, Arizona (Cardinals)

46. What Big Ten team is dubbed the "Buckeyes"?

47. In 2002, what pro football player surpassed Walter Payton's record as the NFL's all-time rushing leader?

48. The NCAA hosts the annual Motor City Bowl in what city?

53

49. What 2000 movie stars Denzel Washington as the African-American coach of a high school football team during its first racially integrated season?

50. In which city does the NCAA host the annual Cotton Bowl?

51. What is it called when a quarterback runs around to avoid the pass rush: scrambling, shuffling or splitting?

54

55

- I was born on February 17, 1936 in Georgia.

- I played nine seasons for the Cleveland Browns.

- I won two MVP Awards: in 1958 and 1965.

- I retired from football when I was 30 years old.

- I've been called the greatest running back in history.

- I was in the movie *The Dirty Dozen*.

I AM JIM BROWN.

AMERICAN
FOOTBALL CONFERENCE

BENGALS	JAGUARS
BILLS	JETS
BRONCOS	PATRIOTS
BROWNS	RAIDERS
CHARGERS	RAVENS
CHIEFS	STEELERS
COLTS	TEXANS
DOLPHINS	TITANS

56

Search for the words listed in all CAPS.

```
              C N X
            Q X R V N Y L
          I C K R T S R U Q K A
        G K S F C I N K Y Q Q U T
        J G X P L O E W F M D S B K K
      B E N G A L S O C N O R B S P
    W E S Q S B T I R Q Q L H X Y B K
    X X W N F E S R B G K P G H R R R
  X G U S T E J J N I K X H P B E R P N
  K Y U T L I V L C G O I I G D W M K R      57
  G G H E J H T A R M K T N G H T Q W Q
    T R X Z C H A R G E R S K Q E O O
    S R A U G A J N G H L B U M B C G
      R N I I E F Q S L C Y Y P Z M
      H S I D Y D M A A M J Y H Y Z
        T F I E V O T I K L Z E K
        O M Q R B K V R L R I
            R P S J H N Y
              F E U
```

52. TV sportscaster Frank Gifford was a running back for what NFL team?

53. What is it called when the center hands the ball to the quarterback?

54. What quarterback married a morning talk show co-host (and former *Survivor* contestant) in 2002?

58

ALIAS SMITH AND JONES

One Monday night, Big Daddy felt like watching a western on TV, but all he could find was a football game. He smiled when he saw the game.

What two teams were playing?

60

Dallas Cowboys vs.
Washington Redskins

or

Dallas Cowboys vs.
Kansas City Chiefs

55. Who was the first athlete to become an all-star in two professional sports?

56. Archie Griffin, the only two-time winner of the Heisman Trophy, played for what Big Ten school?

57. What NFL team is sometimes referred to by fans and sportswriters as the "Big Bay Blues" or "Bays"?

62

- I was born on July 25, 1954 in Columbia, MS.

- I was voted into nine Pro Bowls.

- The Bears drafted me in 1975.

- I scored 125 touchdowns in my NFL career—110 of them rushing.

- I beat both Jim Brown and Frank Harris's rushing records.

- I was named NFL player of the year in 1977 and 1985.

I AM WALTER PAYTON.

- I was born in Pittsburgh in 1961.

- My father and I have the same name, but I don't add "Jr." to mine.

- I threw the most passes of anyone in NFL history, including 420 touchdown passes.

- I began my career in 1983, playing in Miami.

- I was selected for nine Pro Bowls in a row.

- In 2005, I was inducted into the Pro Football Hall of Fame.

I AM DAN MARINO.

58. The colors of the Pittsburgh Steelers' helmet logo symbolize the three materials needed to produce what?

59. The film *Brian's Song* is based on the true story of Brian Piccolo and Gale Sayers, who both played for what pro football team?

60. Pro football player Andre "Bad Moon" Rison's nickname is borrowed from the popular song by what famous band?

Solutions:
58. Steel (yellow for coal, orange for ore and blue for steel scrap)
59. The Chicago Bears 60. Creedence Clearwater Revival

PRIME TIME

In 1989, Deion Sanders became the first professional athlete to play in an NFL Football game and a Major League Baseball game in the same week.

Name the two teams "Neon Deion" played for.

65

Atlanta Falcons (NFL) and
NY Yankees (MLB)

61. What was Jim Otto's jersey number when he played for the Oakland Raiders?

62. What is the playful nickname for women's flag football?

63. How many seams does a regulation football have: 2, 4 or 12?

64. Doug Flutie's famous "Hail Mary" pass was thrown against what losing team?

65. Jane Seymour and Bert Convy star in a 1979 made-for-TV movie about a reporter who goes undercover as a cheerleader for what NFL squad?

66. What former NFL quarterback was the New York Yankees' first pick in the 1981 summer draft?

Solutions:
64. Miami Hurricanes 65. Dallas Cowboy Cheerleaders 66. John Elway

- I was born in Brooklyn in 1913.

- My last coaching job was for the 1969 Washington Redskins.

- I was the NFL's Man of the Decade for the 1960s.

- My Packers won five NFL titles and the first two Super Bowls.

- If you remember Bart Starr and Ray Nitschke, you remember me.

- In my entire NFL coaching career, I never had a losing season.

69

I AM VINCE LOMBARDI.

NATIONAL
FOOTBALL CONFERENCE

BEARS

BUCCANEERS

CARDINALS

COWBOYS

EAGLES

FALCONS

FORTY-NINERS

GIANTS

LIONS

PACKERS

PANTHERS

RAMS

REDSKINS

SAINTS

SEAHAWKS

VIKINGS

70

Search for the words listed in all CAPS.

```
            I V E
          V G W V I D B
        T E W S D Q C K O X W
      F S E E R R M H L I G J T
    W S Y L E E D E Q P U N F U B
    B X G D A E D D H C X D G Y B
  G X A S R E N I N Y T R O F S P O
  I E K R N S A I N T S N O E U W P
O A I K P W O C R D S E R A D P R I L
N N H M W J M C O Z R B H P P N J Z Z    71
S T H V U B I U L K Q A B A E D Q V D
  S R K L W F B K A W Q C Q I R G Z
  X L S Q I L U B K F K U K S M W T
    C O W B O Y S Q E T V W Y G L
    E G M B Z N G R X S I Q X V H
      Z Y D F S S M A R L O T V
        Q Y S R T O E E D C U
          E D A F E R B
            O U Z
```

67. In the *Peanuts* series, who pulls the football out from under Charlie Brown's foot right before he tries to kick it?

68. During the 1980s, the Atlanta Falcons' head coach, Jerry Glanville, had will-call tickets to every home game reserved for what deceased entertainer?

69. Which team did John Heisman coach to college football's National Championship: Notre Dame, Georgia Tech or Stanford?

Solutions:
67. Lucy 68. Elvis Presley 69. Georgia Tech

FAME GAME

Change either the first name or the last name of each of the celebrities below to create two members of the NFL Hall of Fame.

1. Bart Simpson
2. Barry White
3. Woody Allen
4. Sid Caesar

1. Bart Starr, O.J. Simpson
2. Barry Sanders, Randy White
3. George Allen, Marcus Allen
4. Sid Gillman, Sid Luckman

70. In yards, what is the width of a football field: $50\frac{1}{3}$, $53\frac{1}{3}$ or $63\frac{1}{3}$?

71. Who recorded "The Super Bowl Shuffle" in 1985?

72. How many NFL teams are named after cats: two, four or six?

75

Solutions:
70. $53\frac{1}{3}$ 71. The Chicago Bears 72. Four (The Carolina Panthers, the Detroit Lions, the Cincinnati Bengals and the Jacksonville Jaguars)

76

- I graduated from Notre Dame in 1979.

- I missed the entire 1999 season because of injury.

- During my playing days, I was partial to rice.

- I pioneered the West Coast Offense when I played for a West Coast team.

- I won four Super Bowls during the 1980s.

- I finished my career as a Chief in 1994.

I AM JOE MONTANA.

77

- I played my entire career with the same team.

- The Colts picked me first in the 1983 draft.

- I quarterbacked for Stanford University in college.

- The 1980s and 1990s were my decades.

- I threw for 300 touchdowns in my career.

- I won Super Bowl XXXIII with Denver.

I AM JOHN ELWAY.

THEY CALL ME
THE REFRIGERATOR

Andre "BAD MOON" Rison

"BROADWAY" Joe Namath

Charlie "BOWLING BALL" Tollar

Craig "IRONHEAD" Heyward

Daryl "MOOSE" Johnston

Deion "PRIME TIME" Sanders

Dick "NIGHT TRAIN" Lane

Earl "CURLY" Lambeau

Earl "GREASY" Neale

Elroy "CRAZY LEGS" Hirsch

Frank "BRUISER" Kinard

Harold "GALLOPING GHOST" Grange

Jack "HACKSAW" Reynolds

Jack "the ASSASSIN" Tatum

Jerome "the BUS" Bettis

Jim "CAPT. COMEBACK" Harbaugh

Kordell "SLASH" Stewart

"MEAN" Joe Greene

Norman "BOOMER" Esiason

Steve "AIR" McNair

Ted "MAD STORK" Hendricks

Terrell "TD" Davis

Walter "SWEETNESS" Payton

William "the REFRIGERATOR" Perry

78

Search for the words listed in all CAPS.

```
                    I   U   E
                K   H   R   X   A   G   D
            S   E   A   B   O   K   V   Y   C   V   L
        B   N   C   S   W   N   N   X   B   X   F   K   L
    L   U   K   P   B   Z   H   F   Q   A   T   X   R   U   C
    S   S   M   I   R   H   E   F   R   D   S   T   O   U   R
V   A   W   N   B   K   C   A   B   E   M   O   C   T   P   A   C
W   O   E   R   C   F   Z   D   I   F   O   H   Z   S   I   Z   U
I   V   E   E   H   R   R   T   W   R   O   G   K   D   U   Y   R   I
A   O   K   T   S   S   B   O   W   L   I   N   G   B   A   L   L   E
N   Q   M   N   I   A   R   T   T   H   G   I   N   T   M   Q   E   Y   M
    I   P   E   U   L   E   M   I   T   E   M   I   R   P   M   G   B
    L   S   S   R   S   M   E   T   I   R   S   P   I   T   L   S   E
        F   S   B   R   O   A   D   W   A   Y   O   V   Y   J   Y
        I   J   A   X   O   N   D   Q   T   E   L   O   F   C   S
            Y   Z   S   B   O   Y   N   O   Y   L   A   M   M
                E   E   S   C   Q   G   R   E   A   S   Y
                    F   A   U   B   K   Z   G
                        A   D   D
```

73. What colorful name is given to a college player who is kept out of competition for a year without losing his playing eligibility?

74. How many teams play in college football's Big 10 Conference?

75. What is the term for the amount of time a punted ball stays in the air?

80

VERBAL ABUSE

Goofy Gertrude always mixes up the names of her favorite quarterbacks.

Who is she really talking about when she says that she likes Tim Brody, Danny Salt-n-Pepper and Burt Favor?

Tom Brady, Dante Culpepper
and Brett Favre

76. What does the "AC" in A.C. Green stand for: Arthur Clay, Adele Corningsmouth or nothing?

77. What actress did Jason Sehorn marry in 2001?

78. How many minutes of play are in a regulation football game?

79. Doug Williams was the first African-American starting quarterback in a Super Bowl in what year: 1978, 1988 or 1998?

80. With 6,082 yards, Tony Dorsett set what collegiate record from 1973 to 1976?

81. American football traces its origins to what two other sports?

84

- I was born in 1959, and I weighed 237 pounds in 1988.

- I played my entire career with the New York Giants.

- I'm outgoing, but at work I was very defensive.

- I was the NFL Defensive Player of the Year in 1981, 1982 and 1986.

- Linebacker is my favorite position.

- My nickname is "L.T."

85

I AM LAWRENCE TAYLOR.

BROTHERS
IN ARMS

Bart STARR	Phil SIMMS
Brett FAVRE	Roger STAUBACH
Dan FOUTS	Sammy BAUGH
Dan MARINO	Sonny JURGENSEN
Doug FLUTIE	Steve DEBERG
Fran TARKENTON	Steve YOUNG
Jim KELLY	Terry BRADSHAW
Joe NAMATH	Tom BRADY
John ELWAY	Troy AIKMAN
Johnny UNITAS	Vinny TESTAVERDE
Otto GRAHAM	Warren MOON
Peyton MANNING	Y.A. TITTLE

Search for the words listed in all CAPS.

```
            A  L  C
         J  O  H  D  H  Q  C
      P  R  R  B  L  M  T  M  O  N  W
      N  R  Y  W  M  R  T  B  E  A  N  O  O
   M  G  O  Y  H  U  Q  F  L  M  N  H  W  M  S
   X  U  L  Y  P  T  I  X  K  S  O  V  A  G  P
U  N  L  I  A  A  K  O  I  X  U  T  N  H  R  Y  M
G  J  E  S  N  X  W  A  U  E  A  N  K  S  R  G  O
O  V  F  K  S  E  Q  F  L  U  T  I  E  Y  D  A  R  B  Q
F  I  S  A  Q  N  T  I  B  E  N  L  K  H  A  T  B  G  K
Y  L  A  S  V  A  E  Q  M  G  L  H  R  V  R  S  W  T  H
   C  T  X  E  R  P  G  A  Y  S  T  A  U  B  A  C  H
   S  G  R  E  B  E  D  R  E  V  A  T  S  E  T  Q  J
      V  Z  T  V  G  H  I  U  S  M  M  I  S  I  M
      O  I  L  R  W  G  N  B  J  A  Y  V  T  N  K
         R  O  S  T  U  O  F  K  N  Q  W  K  U
         Z  V  K  A  O  T  O  J  Z  N  G
            T  B  M  Z  G  R  B
               P  O  I
```

82. What college's team mascot is a Longhorn steer named Bevo?

83. What was star running back Walter Payton's sugarcoated nickname?

84. Which of these quarterbacks holds the San Francisco 49ers highest career pass rating: Steve Young or Joe Montana?

88

SKYPIECE SABBATH

What distinctive article of clothing did Vince Lombardi and Tom Landry both wear on Sundays during their coaching careers?

89

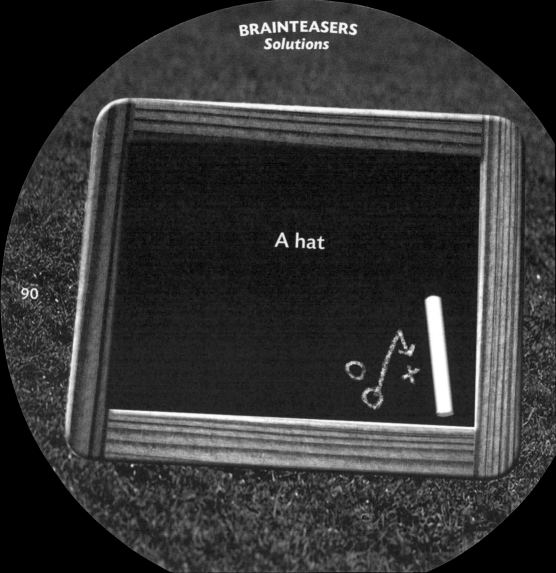

A hat

85. The short-lived USFL lasted for how many seasons: three, four or five?

86. Who is the oldest player to score a Super Bowl touchdown?

87. *Monday Night Football* debuted on ABC in 1970, with Keith Jackson, Don Meredith and who else giving pithy play-by-play?

92

- I was "in the Navy" before I was in the NFL.

- I was the 1963 Heisman Trophy winner.

- I was the MVP in Super Bowl VI.

- I was a four-time NFL passing leader during the 1970s.

- I played my entire career with the same team.

- My coach was Tom Landry.

I AM ROGER STAUBACH.

93

- I was born in California in 1931.

- My 1978 Stanford team played in the Sun Bowl.

- Don Coryell was one of my mentors when I coached in San Diego.

- I coached the 49ers to three Super Bowl titles in 10 years.

- I was 47 when I got my first NFL head coach job.

- I was the NFL's Coach of Year in 1981.

I AM BILL WALSH.

88. What comedian and former *Saturday Night Live* star signed on to co-host *Monday Night Football* in 2000?

89. In February 2002, what football team won a Super Bowl for the first time in the history of its franchise?

94

90. What player went to Super Bowl XXIX with the San Francisco 49ers and then appeared in a Dallas Cowboy uniform in Super Bowl XXX one year later?

TBD (TO BE DETERMINED)

During the Eagles football games in 2005, what were TD, TO and TP?

96

TD: Touchdown
TO: Terrell Owens
TP: Toilet paper

91. What Midwestern team has been defeated twice by the San Francisco 49ers in the Super Bowl?

92. How did the original Cleveland Browns get their name?

93. In 1948, what NFL team became the first to use a team insignia or logo on its helmet?

Solutions:
91. Cincinnati Bengals 92. They were named after legendary coach Paul Brown. 93. The Los Angeles Rams

94. The Steam Roller was an NFL team whose home stadium was the Cyclodome, located in which city?

95. Which official is stationed behind the defensive linemen, on the same side of the field as the wide receiver?

96. What is it called when a play is altered at the line of scrimmage?

98

Solutions:
94. Providence, RI 95. Back Judge 96. Audible

- I was born October 11, 1961.

- My six touchdown throws earned me the MVP title for Super Bowl XXIX.

- I was named All-Pro in 1992, 1993, 1994 and 1998.

- Thanks to my left arm, I won six NFL passing titles.

- I was inducted into the Pro Football Hall of Fame in 2005.

- I'm associated with Utah and Montana.

I AM STEVE YOUNG.

HALL OF FAMERS

Bob GRIESE

Dan DIERDORF

Dan FOUTS

Dan MARINO

Eric DICKERSON

Franco HARRIS

Fritz POLLARD

Gino MARCHETTI

Jim BROWN

Jim THORPE

Joe GREENE

Joe MONTANA

Joe NAMATH

John ELWAY

Johnny UNITAS

Lawrence TAYLOR

Lynn SWANN

Marcus ALLEN

Terry BRADSHAW

Tony DORSETT

100

Search for the words listed in all CAPS.

WORD SEARCHES

```
            T  A  D
         O  N  N  U  K  D  M
      G  C  V  A  O  H  P  I  B  F  S
      Q  O  Z  T  M  S  T  T  E  S  R  O  D
   R  T  M  N  Q  A  R  T  B  R  I  T  O  U  L
   E  G  O  M  D  T  E  H  Q  D  R  A  H  W  T
T  L  M  N  H  N  H  K  O  G  O  R  Y  Y  B  N  S
Q  B  E  I  Y  C  P  C  R  D  R  A  L  L  O  P  J
Z  N  C  R  R  R  Q  X  I  P  U  F  H  O  W  J  M  U  T
A  E  F  X  A  U  F  E  D  E  N  E  E  R  G  W  C  T  M
P  K  I  M  M  D  S  W  L  Q  I  E  O  X  D  Z  J  N  O
   P  M  K  R  E  S  N  U  W  T  I  K  P  L  W  J  K
   D  S  M  Q  C  X  H  I  T  A  T  U  M  H  N  G  Z
      W  Q  R  N  N  A  W  S  Y  Y  P  G  L  B
      C  G  T  W  H  N  L  W  D  F  T  V  I  I  D
         L  A  M  A  O  L  D  W  H  O  H  K  P
         J  M  K  D  E  U  Q  Y  E  K  T
            P  L  N  M  H  Y  G
               T  W  P
```

101

97. How many stadiums had games in progress when the Japanese bombed Pearl Harbor?

98. The game known as "Miracle at the Meadowlands" was played on November 19, 1978 between which two teams?

99. What is the term used when a game isn't televised in the team's hometown?

102

MUCKY MONIKERS

Name the teams associated with these nicknames:

1. The Fearsome Foursome
2. The Purple People Eaters
3. The Hogs
4. The Steel Curtain

103

1. Los Angeles Rams
2. Minnesota Vikings
3. Washington Redskins
4. Pittsburgh Steelers

104

100. What is the slang name for a field's four corners?

101. Pooches and squibs are both types of what?

102. What is the name of the orange markers found in every end zone?

106

- I'm a Baby Boomer from Evansville, Indiana.

- I was All-American twice at Purdue.

- In 1971, I was the NFL's Player of the Year.

- As quarterback, I led my team to victory in Super Bowls VII and VIII.

- I have a son named Brian who is also a Pro Football quarterback.

- My career began and ended with the Dolphins.

I AM BOB GRIESE.

- I was born in Florida and attended college at Florida State.

- In 1990, I was Rookie of the Year.

- Coach Jimmy Johnson drafted me to play with the Dallas Cowboys.

- I rushed for 132 yards and two touchdowns in Super Bowl XXVIII, winning the MVP title.

- I was part of one of the Cowboys' all-time strongest offensive lines.

- I ended my career with the Phoenix Cardinals.

107

I AM EMMITT SMITH.

WIN ONE
FOR THE GIPPER!

Bill BELICHICK	Joe GIBBS
Bill COWHER	John MADDEN
Bill PARCELLS	Knute ROCKNE
Bill WALSH	Marv LEVY
Bud GRANT	Mike DITKA
Chuck NOLL	Paul BROWN
Don SHULA	Paul BRYANT
Eddie ROBINSON	Steve MARIUCCI
George ALLEN	Steve OWEN
George HALAS	Tom FLORES
Hank STRAM	Tom LANDRY
Jimmy JOHNSON	Vince LOMBARDI

108

Search for the words listed in all CAPS.

```
                    I  U  E
                 V  J  B  J  J  O  L
              C  E  N  K  C  O  R  V  X  X  I
           Z  U  N  N  O  L  L  L  K  S  C  R  V
        J  R  Y  Y  W  E  S  A  G  A  C  X  S  Y  Y
        I  C  V  H  O  T  D  N  W  U  R  Q  S  L  H
     V  T  I  E  C  R  Z  G  D  I  T  K  A  L  A  R  D
     Z  A  R  L  A  B  I  D  R  A  B  M  O  L  S  C  T
  P  T  N  D  M  S  B  R  A  Y  E  M  O  A  E  V  N  C  D
  O  T  H  O  X  B  O  M  A  L  U  H  S  R  C  A  T  L  M
  R  T  U  N  S  S  Z  C  I  L  A  S  O  W  R  N  S  Y  M
     A  I  M  K  N  D  C  G  R  N  L  H  G  A  U  N  O
     P  B  W  M  U  H  R  J  L  F  A  L  Y  P  A  W  G
        R  E  D  I  J  O  Z  M  N  W  R  E  O  E  N
        L  O  C  U  C  D  J  R  X  B  K  E  N  Y  C
           K  R  B  K  T  I  M  F  O  E  H  H  A
           H  V  L  Y  D  K  Z  Q  T  I  U
              H  Z  W  G  Q  J  C
                 D  J  F
```

103. The defensive strategy called a "red dog" is also known as what?

104. Who was the first president of the NFL (then called APFA)?

105. Pigskin is an inaccurate and antiquated name for which piece of equipment?

110

Solutions:
103. Blitz. 104. Jim Thorpe. 105. Football

BEST OF THE BEST

What did Steve Largent and Jerry Rice do better than any of their teammates or competitors?

106. What does PAT stand for?

107. What is the status of the ball in-between plays?

108. What do Steve Young, Ken Stabler, Boomer Esiason, Jim Zorn and Frankie Albert all have that Joe Montana doesn't?

113

109. What is the main job of a flanker?

110. Which NFL quarterback was first to pass for 4,000 yards?

111. What is it called when a player throws the ball at the ground after scoring a touchdown?

114

- I attended college at Mississippi Valley State.

- I began my pro football career in 1985 with the 49ers.

- I am the NFL's all-time leading receiver.

- In 1989, I was the Super Bowl MVP.

- After the 1990s, I crossed the Bay to play for Oakland.

- In 2005, I played for the Seattle Seahawks.

I AM JERRY RICE.

MONDAY MORNING
QUARTERBACKS

Al DE ROGATIS

Al MICHAELS

Boomer ESIASON

Brian BALDINGER

Curt GOWDY

Dan FOUTS

Don MEREDITH

Frank GIFFORD

Howard COSELL

Howie LONG

Ian EAGLE

Jim BROWN

Jim GRAY

John DOCKERY

John MADDEN

Keith JACKSON

Marv ALBERT

Matt MILLEN

Pat SUMMERALL

Paul CHRISTMAN

Ron JAWORSKI

Sam ROSEN

Steve YOUNG

Terry BRADSHAW

Search for the words listed in all CAPS.

WORD SEARCHES

```
            W   P   U
        R   A   Q   F   P   M   H
    K   P   O   W   I   S   O   W   P   M   X
  S   Q   D   P   Y   Z   E   J   U   C   I   M   T
R   N   I   X   L   L   L   H   D   H   T   K   U   N   G
V   B   S   T   L   G   R   T   R   B   A   S   M   N   W
B   L   S   L   E   A   H   C   I   M   L   J   R   U   R   P   A
S   R   G   S   E   R   G   S   D   B   D   R   O   F   F   I   G
A   F   Q   O   U   T   E   T   O   E   B   L   Y   W   B   I   R   N   C
B   E   C   W   F   E   M   Q   R   R   X   U   J   A   C   K   S   O   N
C   N   E   D   D   A   M   T   A   E   E   L   L   J   M   O   N   L   F
R   W   Y   N   T   U   D   D   M   S   D   J   V   P   K   C   M
S   A   O   G   E   S   I   D   F   I   I   D   O   Q   S   K   R
    D   I   R   H   S   Q   E   N   A   L   D   Q   H   O   R
    W   I   A   B   I   J   G   M   S   R   L   R   M   O   X
      W   Y   Y   R   E   K   C   O   D   S   E   U   A
        C   O   R   O   S   E   N   L   X   C   N
          B   Y   H   K   K   F   T
            F   D   O
```

112. Which football team still holds the record set in 1921-1923 for most games (25) won in a row?

113. What is the name of the official list of team members?

114. What is the name of the team get-together during which the next play is discussed?

Solutions:
112. Canton Bulldogs 113. The roster 114. Huddle

FISH FEATHERS

The Marks Brothers played for the Miami Dolphins during the 1970s.

What are their last names?

119

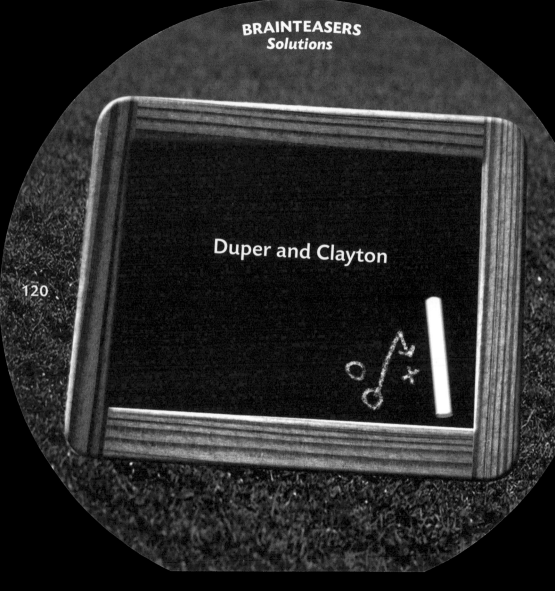

115. Which team was the first wildcard team to reach a Super Bowl?

116. What is the name of the play right after a touchdown in which a team can try to earn two extra points from their opponent's two-yard line?

117. Who was the first defensive player to be named the NFL Player of the year?

122

- I was born December 5, 1947.

- In 1970, I won the Heisman Trophy while attending Stanford.

- I was named the AFC's Rookie of the Year while playing with the New England Patriots.

- I led the Raiders to a 38-9 victory over the Redskins in Super Bowl XVIII.

- The 49ers had me as a quarterback for two years before I went to the Raiders.

- I was the 1981 Super Bowl MVP.

I AM JIM PLUNKETT.

• I was born in
Norway in 1888.

• In 13 years of coaching
the same college team,
we lost only 12 games —
a record for both
college and pro teams.

• I coached the "Gipper."

• I spent 1918 to 1931 in
South Bend with the
Fighting Irish.

• ESPN named me #10 on
their SportsCentury's
Greatest Coaches list.

• My Four Horsemen were
unstoppable.

I AM KNUTE ROCKNE.

118. What is the name of the folks who help the officials by measuring the first down?

119. During which year did the Miami Dolphins play the NFL's first perfect season?

120. In football, a "sack" is made when a QB is tackled where?

124

BEARLY LEGAL

During the early 1980s, Pete Oatman bet Andy Snow that he could take him to a place where 50,000 people paid money to watch a refrigerator run.

Who won the bet?

125

126

Pete did. (He took Andy to Soldier Field to watch William "the Refrigerator" Perry play for the Chicago Bears.)

121. Merlin and Phil Olsen are brothers who spent four years playing together on what team?

122. The metal rod with a box on top, used to keep track of the down being played, is called what?

123. Who won the 1967 Super Bowl known as the Ice Bowl, in which temperatures dropped to 13 degrees below zero?

Solutions:
121. Los Angeles Rams 122. Down box 123. Green Bay Packers (over the Dallas Cowboys)

124. What is the projected difference in points scored between two teams in an upcoming game?

125. Which team did Johnny Unitas play for when he retired?

126. As of the beginning of the 2005 season, who held the NFL record for the most touchdowns in his rookie season?

Solutions:
124. Point spread 125. The San Diego Chargers (in 1972)
126. Gale Sayers, 1965

- When I was born in 1962, I was named "Vincent."

- I turned down the Yankees for a football scholarship at Auburn.

- In 1985, I won the Heisman Trophy.

- I was elected to the National Football Foundation and College Hall of Fame in 1999.

- I am the only athlete ever to be voted to All-Star games in two major professional sports.

- Who knows about football and baseball? I know.

129

I AM BO JACKSON.

FLEA FLICKERS

ALL THE RIGHT MOVES	REMEMBER THE TITANS
ANY GIVEN SUNDAY	RUDY
BRIAN'S SONG	The BEST OF TIMES
FRIDAY NIGHT LIGHTS	The LONGEST YARD
JERRY MAGUIRE	The REPLACEMENTS
NECESSARY ROUGHNESS	VARSITY BLUES
NORTH DALLAS FORTY	WATER BOY
RADIO	WILDCATS

Search for the words listed in all CAPS.

```
            G O Q
          F D H X E L P
        S T A C D L I W G Q S
      R E P L A C E M E N T S L
    I P S E U L B Y T I S R A V H
    U M E J X X Y O B R E T A W M
  F R I D A Y N I G H T L I G H T S
  R E M E M B E R T H E T I T A N S
S S E N H G U O R Y R A S S E C E N T
S E V O M T H G I R E H T L L A E C E
P L Y T R O F S A L L A D H T R O N L
  L U A N Y G I V E N S U N D A Y T
  C V T L R E R I U G A M Y R R E J
    B E S T O F T I M E S R A L E
    D R A Y T S E G N O L D J R O
    N U G N O S S N A I R B B F
      D D H B F W Z O T Z O
        Y E V M O N U
          T V J
```

131

127. In what year did it become legal to make a forward pass from anywhere behind the line of scrimmage: 1933, 1953 or 1973?

128. On March 25, 1971, what NFL team changed their name to the New England Patriots?

129. In what year was the head slap officially outlawed: 1974, 1977 or 1980?

NEVER MORE

Name the 19th century poet whose favorite football team plays in Baltimore.

Edgar Allen Poe
(He wrote "The Raven.")

130. What University of Chicago Heisman Trophy winner became the first player ever to be drafted to the NFL, but opted not to turn pro?

131. In 1943 the NFL made mandatory the use of what piece of protective equipment?

132. What former Baltimore Colt was the first full-time offensive lineman to be elected to the Football Hall of Fame?

Solutions:
130. Jay Berwanger 131. The helmet 132. Jim Parker (in 1973)

136

- I played quarterback for the Raiders during the 1970s.

- In 1976, I was the NFL's Player of the Year and Passing Champion.

- I played the Pro Bowl in 1973, '74 and '76.

- Scotch was my drink of choice.

- I was the last recipient of the multi-sport Hickock Belt Trophy.

- In 1977, I led the Oakland Raiders to their first ever Super Bowl Championship.

I AM KENNY STABLER.

- I was born in Texas in 1926 and attended college at Louisiana State.

- My first name is Yelberton.

- The NFL named me MVP in 1961 and 1963.

- During my 17-season career as a quarterback, I played for the Baltimore Colts, the San Francisco 49ers and the New York Giants.

- While playing for the Giants, I threw 33 touch-down passes in 1962 and 36 in 1963.

- I was elected to seven Pro Bowls.

I AM Y.A. TITTLE

GOLDEN RECEIVERS

Amani TOOMER

Art MONK

Bobby MITCHELL

Cris CARTER

Deion BRANCH

Isaac BRUCE

Jerry RICE

John STALLWORTH

Lynn SWANN

Marvin HARRISON

Michael IRVING

Paul WARFIELD

Raymond BERRY

Terrell OWENS

Troy BROWN

Wayne CHREBET

Search for the words listed in all CAPS.

WORD SEARCHES

```
            H  J  W
         P  D  T  B  G  Q  L
      U  D  C  A  R  T  E  R  C  D  C
   W  C  N  K  N  O  M  C  R  P  H  T  T
X  F  U  S  W  G  W  I  U  B  R  O  W  N  S
G  H  U  Q  R  D  L  S  R  E  O  Y  T  L  J
Y  V  S  J  X  E  H  L  L  B  M  H  M  M  U  O  A
N  E  N  S  R  E  F  A  E  E  W  R  D  D  W  S  U
D  Z  A  N  R  I  N  L  T  R  I  H  V  H  J  I  U  V  I
O  I  J  E  N  N  A  W  S  I  R  F  C  B  U  Q  Q  P  G
L  R  V  T  E  J  D  W  C  C  V  I  R  T  K  Z  L  D  J
V  E  X  U  D  G  Q  P  E  I  A  S  A  I  J  I  G
E  T  H  I  D  M  V  P  S  N  E  W  O  W  M  L  O
   L  H  G  G  R  B  C  C  G  F  F  U  N  X  C
   O  I  Y  C  S  X  H  A  T  F  W  G  T  N  X
      E  V  O  S  N  I  B  M  Z  F  F  Y  W
         O  M  T  U  N  V  F  V  W  B  B
            F  C  O  Z  W  W  L
               S  B  Z
```

133. In 1986, NFL owners accepted what tool for limited use by officials to call games with greater accuracy?

134. Who was the first African-American head coach in the NFL?

135. After a league record 26 consecutive losses, what team did the Tampa Bay Buccaneers beat on December 11, 1977 for their first NFL win?

140

SMILE WHEN YOU SAY THAT

Goofy Gertrude is all mixed up again. She thinks that she wants autographs from Joan Ebay, Kent Stapler, Carry Bradshaw and Stan Marina.

Which quarterbacks is she really looking for?

John Elway, Ken Stabler,
Terry Bradshaw and Dan Marino

136. Who was the first left-handed quarterback to be inducted to the Hall of Fame?

137. Name one of the three players who share the record of three fumbles in a single Super Bowl game.

138. As of the start of the 2005 season, what NFL team had the most regular season wins?

Solutions:
136. Steve Young (in 2005) 137. Roger Staubach (Super Bowl X); Jim Kelly (Super Bowl XXVII); Frank Reich (Super Bowl XXVIII)
138. The Chicago Bears (with 646)

139. With his February 2005 win, how many Super Bowl rings did Tom Brady have?

140. What tie-settling rule was used for the first time on August 28, 1954 to end a game between the Rams and the Giants?

141. What famous Jazz Singer sang the National Anthem at Super Bowl XXI on January 25, 1987?

144

- Shreveport is my hometown and I attended Louisiana Tech.

- I was the NFL MVP in 1978.

- I played quarterback for the Pittsburgh Steelers from 1970 to 1983.

- Lynn Swann was my receiver.

- I led my team to four Super Bowl Championships, passing for a total of 932 yards and nine touchdowns.

- I was named MVP in two Super Bowls, XIII and XIV.

145

I AM TERRY BRADSHAW.

BABY GOT BACK

Brian DAWKINS (defensive back)

Champ BAILEY (defensive back)

Charles WOODSON (defensive back)

Deion SANDERS (defensive back)

Dick LANE (defensive back)

Jack TATUM (defensive back)

Mel BLOUNT (defensive back)

Rodney HARRISON (defensive back)

Samari ROLLE (defensive back)

Ty LAW (defensive back)

Barry SANDERS (running back)

Corey DILLON (running back)

Curtis MARTIN (running back)

Earl CAMPBELL (running back)

Jerome BETTIS (running back)

Jim BROWN (running back)

Jim TAYLOR (running back)

Paul HORNUNG (running back)

Ricky WILLIAMS (running back)

Walter PAYTON (running back)

Search for the words listed in all CAPS.

```
            O  L  H
         Z  N  Z  O  X  L  B
      G  N  U  N  R  O  H  E  N  Q  J
   B  S  J  O  O  F  H  C  Z  G  P  G  L
   W  N  N  D  A  S  T  T  O  N  J  P  D  B  V
   E  W  I  L  L  I  A  M  S  H  S  B  A  Q  L
N  O  G  K  T  R  R  T  N  O  L  L  I  D  Y  P  L
R  O  W  W  A  R  R  U  X  D  T  L  Z  D  F  T  M
B  F  S  S  A  Y  C  A  M  P  B  E  L  L  O  R  N  O  B
M  N  Y  C  D  L  Q  H  M  Q  Y  E  R  A  Q  O  U  Z  N
Y  V  E  Z  D  O  P  Y  I  L  P  B  T  S  N  H  O  V  J
Y  H  R  J  R  O  D  B  Z  A  F  O  T  U  E  L  J
W  O  A  E  M  T  W  F  E  K  L  C  N  I  H  B  C
   A  C  D  H  U  I  X  D  S  A  E  C  U  S  J
   D  A  S  S  J  Y  A  R  R  P  J  Z  R  S  K
      B  G  G  V  N  U  L  K  I  T  G  Y  X
         Z  X  N  Q  Q  K  P  M  D  J  W
            Z  R  H  L  J  B  N
               L  Q  E
```

147

142. In what year will Super Bowl L be held?

143. What running back completed the famous "Immaculate Reception," giving the Steelers their first ever postseason win?

144. On June 24, 1922, the name National Football League was adopted to replace what moniker?

Solutions:
142. 2016 143. Franco Harris (in 1972, 13-7 over the Raiders) 144. American Professional Football Association

NICKNAME NONSENSE

By what names were these players and coaches better known?

1. The Snake
2. Mooch
3. The Galloping Ghost
4. Johnny U

1. Ken Stabler
2. Steve Mariucci
3. Red Grange
4. Johhny Unitas

WORD SEARCHES
Solutions

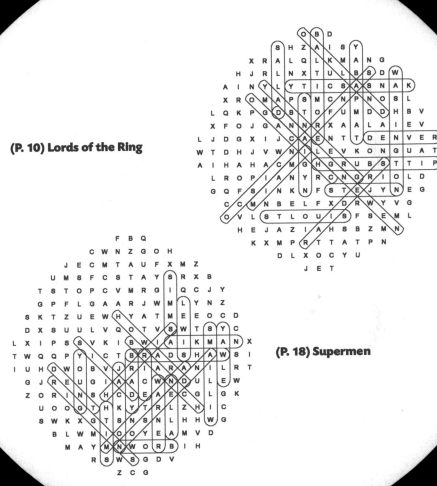

(P. 10) Lords of the Ring

(P. 18) Supermen

151

WORD SEARCHES
Solutions

(P. 26) If They Could See Me Now

152

(P. 40) You Make the Call!

WORD SEARCHES
Solutions

(P. 48) Not in Our House!

(P. 56) American Football Conference

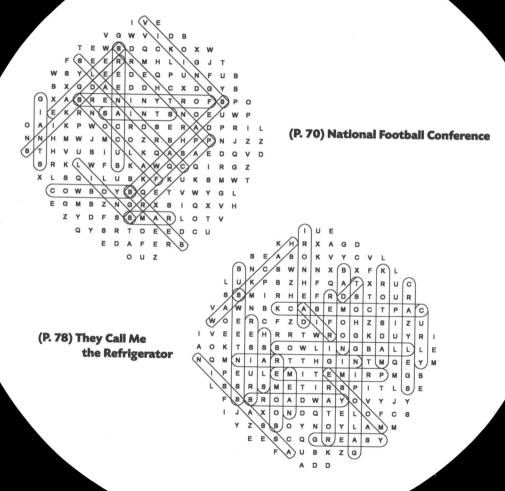

(P. 70) National Football Conference

(P. 78) They Call Me the Refrigerator

154

WORD SEARCHES
Solutions

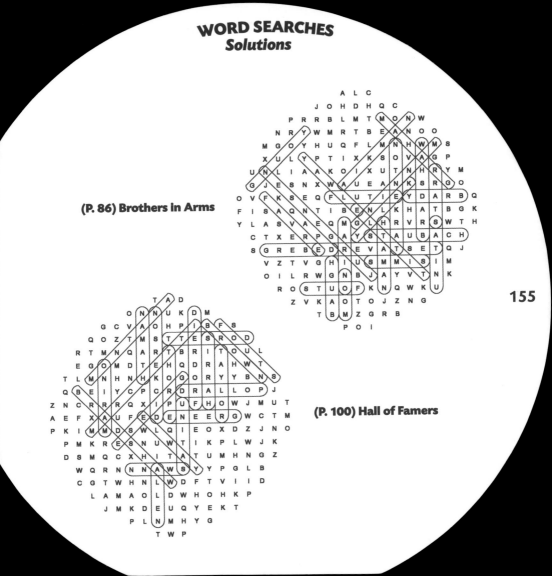

(P. 86) Brothers in Arms

(P. 100) Hall of Famers

WORD SEARCHES
Solutions

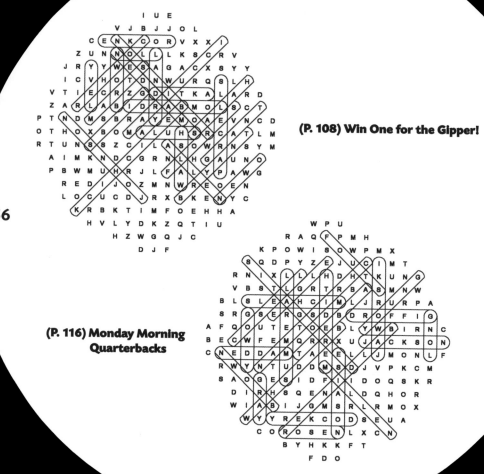

(P. 108) Win One for the Gipper!

(P. 116) Monday Morning Quarterbacks

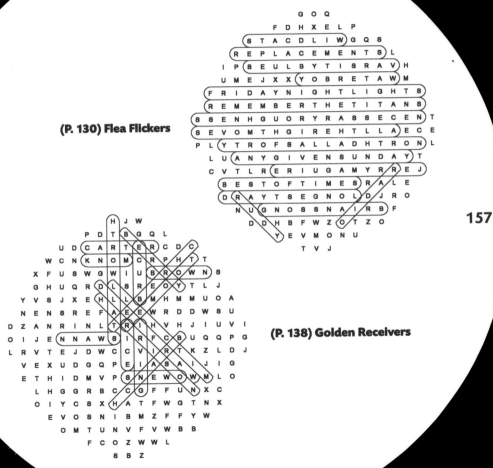

(P. 130) Flea Flickers

(P. 138) Golden Receivers

158

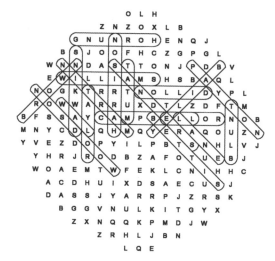

(P. 146) Baby Got Back

INDEX

Bob Moog, co-founder of University Games, has been creating games, brainteasers, word puzzles and the like since childhood. The Ball Busters™ series is his first foray into mixing his love of games with his passion for sports. In this series, he shares more than 40 years of his own arcane knowledge about sports, along with some interesting tidbits pried from colleagues and family.